Hiking

BY ALLAN MOREY

AMICUS HIGH INTEREST • AMICUS INK

Amicus High Interest and Amicus Ink are imprints of Amicus
P.O. Box 1329, Mankato, MN 56002
www.amicuspublishing.us

Library of Congress Cataloging-in-Publication Data
Morey, Allan.
 Hiking / by Allan Morey.
    pages cm – (Great Outdoors)
 Includes index.
 Summary: "This photo-illustrated book for elementary students
describes hikes from a simple nature walk to a miles-long
trek across rough terrain. Includes information on safety and
equipment needed"– Provided by publisher.
 ISBN 978-1-60753-800-4 (library binding)
 ISBN 978-1-68151-020-0 (ebook)
 ISBN 978-1-68152-079-7 (pbk.)
 1. Hiking–Juvenile literature. I. Title.
 GV199.52.M67 2017
 796.51–dc23

                          2015023968

Editor: Wendy Dieker
Series Designer: Kathleen Petelinsek
Book Designer: Tracy Myers
Photo Researchers: Derek Brown and Rebecca Bernin

Photo Credits: Dusan Zidar / Shutterstock cover; Monkey
Business Images, Ltd / Dreamstime 5, Anton Gvozdikov
/ Shutterstock 6, THPStock / Shutterstock 9, Maridav /
Shutterstock 10, Terry Vine / Blend Images / Corbis 13,
TDway / Shutterstock 14-15, Jesse Kunerth / Shutterstock 17,
absolut images / Shutterstock 18, Blue Jean Images / Corbis
21, wong yu liang / Shutterstock 22, Hurst Photo / Shutterstock
25, Maksym Gorpenyuk / Shutterstock 26, Hero Images, Inc. /
Corbis 28-29

Printed in the United States of America.

HC 10 9 8 7 6 5 4 3 2 1
PB 10 9 8 7 6 5 4 3 2 1

Table of Contents

Let's Go Hiking

Imagine you hear birds chirping. You smell wildflowers in the air. A dirt path crunches under your feet. Your family is walking by your side. They are laughing and telling stories. You are out exploring. You aren't just walking around. You are hiking.

A hike doesn't have to be hard work. Hikers can explore an easy trail over a short distance.

Some hikers carry camping and climbing gear for a long hike in the mountains.

Q How long does it take to hike the American Discovery Trail?

Hiking is a great sport for getting outdoors. You can explore a local park. You might trek through the woods. Some hikers climb mountains.

Hikes can be short. Or they can be very long. Some hikers go for months! The American Discovery Trail covers more than 6,800 miles (10,900 km) from California to Maryland. It is the longest hiking trail in the United States.

 One couple spent over a year hiking the trail. They took two breaks. One break was about four months. The other was about one month.

What Hikers Need

Hikers must keep their feet comfortable. On most hikes, they only need a good pair of sneakers. But some paths are steep and rocky. Then they need shoes or boots with a lot of **tread**. Soles with good tread grip the ground really well. Other trails are close to the water. Then waterproof boots are a good idea.

Serious hikers choose hiking boots with good ankle support.

A jacket keeps this hiker warm and dry on a mountain hike.

 Can you hike in the snow?

The weather can change quickly on a long hike. Hikers dress for all kinds of weather. They dress in layers. They may wear a jacket over a sweatshirt, and wear a t-shirt under the sweatshirt. If they get warm, they take off a layer. A hat shades their eyes on a sunny day. A poncho keeps them dry in case it rains.

 Yes! Just wear snowshoes. They keep you from sinking into the snow.

For a short hike, hikers may not need much. But for an all-day trip, they may bring a backpack. Then they can carry water and snacks. They may even bring extra clothes.

A map is also good to have in a new area. A trail map shows the twists and turns of a trail. It also shows sights to see on a hike.

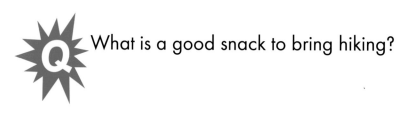 What is a good snack to bring hiking?

**These hikers study the map.
Should they go north?**

 Trail mix. It is a mix of nuts and dried fruit. These foods give you lots of energy and are easy to pack.

There are many other things hikers can take with them. If the trail is hilly, hikers might use **hiking poles**. These sticks help hikers keep their balance.

Do they want to bird watch? Then they need a pair of **binoculars**. Do they want to show people what they saw? Then they bring a camera.

Hiking poles help prevent falls on uneven ground.

Safety First

An important part of hiking is keeping safe. Always tell someone where you are going—even if you are just at a local park. If something happens, people will know where to look for you.

On the trails, always read the signs. They are there to help you. The signs will keep you from getting lost. They will also tell you of any dangers.

A sign helps hikers know where the trail is. It might be unsafe to go off the trail.

STAY
ON
TRAIL

17913-38493

VOSS SIGN, MANLIUS, NY 13104-0553   1-800-473-0691

The outdoors is filled with creatures. Some are tiny, like wood ticks. Others are large, like bears. For the small critters, use bug spray. For large animals, make noise as you walk. Then the animals know where you are. They will usually try to stay away. Most animals are only dangerous if you surprise them.

Bug spray helps stop bugs from biting. A bad bite can ruin a good hike.

A prepared hiker carries a **survival kit**. For short hikes, you only need simple items. Start with a first aid kit. It should have bandages for cuts or blisters. For longer hikes, add a compass, snacks, and a bottle of water.

Another good item to carry is a whistle. If you get lost, blow the whistle. Three short blasts tell people you need help.

Q What should I do if I get lost?

Cuts can happen on a hike. These hikers were ready with a bandage.

 Stay put. Walking around makes it harder for people to find you. Let the rescuers come to you.

A family explores a park on a hike through the city.

Q Can I hike in a city?

Where to Go

Hikes do not need to be long wilderness adventures. Many places are great for hiking. Start with a short hike. Walk the paths at a local park. You can hike anywhere. Just get out and explore. That is what hiking is all about. After a few short trips, you can plan longer hikes.

Yes! Try **urban hiking**. Hike on sidewalks, find pedestrian trails, and explore old railroad yards. Just keep to city property.

Next, go to a **state park**. Some have miles and miles of trails. Their paths may go through forests and swamps. Some have lakes and mountains to explore. Many also have campsites. If you can't hike all of the paths in one day, camp at the park. That will give you the chance to stomp around more of the park's trails.

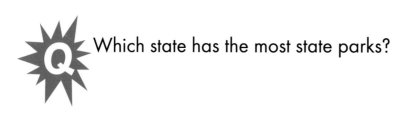
Which state has the most state parks?

An adventurous hike can take you over fallen tree trunks. Step carefully!

 California does. Hikers can find 4,500 miles (7,242 km) of trails in these state parks.

A hike up a mountain means lots of gear. But this hiker is rewarded with a great view!

Q Which state has the most national parks?

A **backcountry hike** can last for days. Some areas might not have a real trail to follow. You can blaze your own path! Large **national parks** are great for backcountry hiking. These trips let you visit places that most people never get to see. But this kind of hiking is only for experienced hikers. It is hard work!

 Alaska. More than 2 million people visit these 23 parks each year.

Have Fun!

Hiking can be a lot of fun. You may see new sights. You might spot animals and flowers that you have never seen before. You will also have stories to tell friends and family. So have fun and go hiking. Explore the world around you. You never know what you will see.

Exploring the great outdoors is good family fun.

Glossary

backcountry hike A hike in an area of few buildings or people; there may be few marked trails and few modern conveniences.

binoculars A tool with magnifying lenses used for seeing objects that are far away.

hiking poles Walking sticks or poles that hikers carry to help them keep balance on rough or hilly ground.

national park A natural area owned by a country that is set aside to be used for recreation.

state park A natural area owned by a state to be used for recreation.

survival kit Emergency supplies, such as food, water, and a first aid kit.

tread The bumps and grooves on the sole of a shoe or boot.

urban hiking Exploring urban areas on foot, usually by finding pedestrian walkways, staircases, and bridges that lead to other parts of the city.

Read More

Champion, Neil. *Wild Trail: Hiking and Camping.* Mankato, MN: Smart Apple Media, 2013.

Time for Kids. *The Book of How: All About Survival.* New York: Time Home Entertainment Inc., 2011.

Websites

Kids Health | Woods and Camping Safety for the Whole Family
kidshealth.org/parent/firstaid_safe/outdoor/woods.html

National Geographic | World's Best Hikes
adventure.nationalgeographic.com/adventure/trips/best-trails/world-hikes/

PBS Kids: Solo Sports | Walking and Hiking
pbskids.org/itsmylife/body/solosports/article6.html

Index

About the Author

Some of Allan Morey's favorite memories from his childhood are camping every summer with his grandparents. While hiking, fishing and camping with them, he grew to enjoy the outdoors. He still does those things, only now he takes his wife and kids with him. They enjoy hiking around the woods too.